CW00502428

AILEEN BALLANTYNE is a national
poet. She was the staff Medical C
Guardian and *The Sunday Times*.
been commended at the British Pr
features on AIDS in *The Sunday Times* won the David Boyle (Erskine Hospital) Memorial Award at the Scottish Press Awards.

Aileen recently completed a PhD in Creative Writing and Modern Poetry at the University of Edinburgh, where she now teaches an undergraduate course on Contemporary Poetry. In 2015, she won first prize in the Mslexia Poetry Competition for her poem on the Lockerbie disaster and the short poem category at the Poetry on the Lake Festival in Orta San Giulio, Italy. She is also a recent winner of the Scots category of the Wigtown Poetry Prize (2012). In 2018, she received the prestigious Scottish Book Trust New Writers' Award.

Taking Flight is her first poetry collection.

Taking Flight

AILEEN BALLANTYNE

To Jimmy & Kitty
from
Aileen Ballantyne
xx

Luath Press Limited
EDINBURGH
www.luath.co.uk

First published 2019

ISBN: 978-1-913025-41-0

The paper used in this book is recyclable. It is made from low chlorine pulps produced in a low energy, low emission manner from renewable forests.

Printed and bound by Bell & Bain Ltd., Glasgow

Typeset in 11 point Sabon by Lapiz

For my son, Alastair

Contents

A Meteor Shower

This is a photograph...

Acknowledgements

My thanks are due to friends and family for their support and, in particular, to the following people and organisations:

To poets Alan Gillis and John Glenday for their wisdom and inspiration at important stages in this project.

To Professor Ian Campbell and Robert Alan Jamieson of the University of Edinburgh's Department of English and Scottish Literature and Creative Writing, for inspiring me to start the journey from journalist to poet in the first place.

To all at Luath Press – my publisher, Gavin MacDougall, for his considerable support and advice, and Maia Gentle for her patience and cover design, and for getting the book to print so quickly.

To my husband Robert – because poetry is all the better for being enjoyed and shared.

To the Scottish Book Trust for their unstinting support and encouragement as part of their New Writers' Award scheme 2018.

Bird of Paradise

Full Moon

The Moon rode with us
all the way from west to east,
so bright at first
I couldn't look.

Here two miles high
in a Boeing Triple Seven,
slowly, my eyes adjusted
to the sheen of it:
a pulsing mirrored circle
alongside me in the dark.

I touched my leather rucksack,
safe beneath my seat,
my mother's necklace,
Blue Grass perfume,
the turquoise ring,
assuring myself I had
all I needed.

Tilted forward in my seatbelt
to the porthole
I gazed full-on
at the great silver disc of the Moon,
the terrible press of thin cold glass
on my forehead.

Knowledge of Starlings: *Stormo di Storni*

Allegretto, *adagio*,
accelerando, *capriccioso*,
the starlings of Rome
know them all
as they write their cantatas
in clear winter skies.

At Stazione Termini today
half a million winged grace notes
fly to the rhythm
of an unseen conductor,
form a panther, a bell-jar, a tree.
Tomorrow, at Piazza Cinquecento,

a lion, a stingray, a fish,
a murmuration that twists,
folds the strands of a double helix
to a hand in the heavens

that tumbles and turns
to a solid black cloud
that covers the sun.

And never a collision
in the rhythm of
their time.

Seven

Project STARFLAG: *'Starlings in Flight', Rome*

The secret of the gathering of the starlings
was hidden in the pulse of a prayer –
whispered each to each in murmurations,

until, with tunnels of wind and each form
and each measure of 3D precision,
the scientists of STARFLAG would fathom
how starlings obtain each decision as one.

But when they unravelled a starling the answer
was a number: the number was seven:
each starling flies forever with seven,

and try as they might, with every algorithm,
the scientists could never explain
how, in half a million, every starling
will find seven again – and again.

Tusitala

'Interviewing' Robert Louis Stevenson

It was not the place of my birth that I loved,
nor the trail of her smoke nor the sun on the Forth,
nor the dark of her light nor her half-light,

but this land I have found
and the splash and the roar of her sea

where the women take the hair from their heads
to weave bamboograss mosaics
and the ink dries on my pen as I write.

I stand now on a hillside
by the sweet vanilla planted
and her people are my people.

I remember, now and then,
the pale light of the north:
its soot-black towers
and razored dusk-black steeples
etched out in silhouette
and the counterpane coughed red
as I lay in bed, dreaming
paper-chains of islands in my head.

It was not the place of my birth that I loved
but this land I have found
where they call me Tusitala
and I breathe with the sea.

After a portrait of RL Stevenson
in Samoa, by Count Girolamo Nerli (1892)

Bird of Paradise

I wanted to capture the gull-throated song,
the red of the lilt of the cardinal's wing,
the sound of his cry in the yellow hibiscus,

the light of a million square diamonds,
the white throbbing heat,
the coral-shaped head of the great cicinnurus.

And so in the cover of darkness
I grasp a long blade,
nick off each foot and the tip of each wing,

wrap him in the leaves of a cool green laburnum,
steal him to circle the haar of my garden.

The Inventor

He longs for the colours
of butterflies' wings –
abalone wings, incandescent
in rainforest light,
wings that shine green
to the eyes of all men –
yet will metamorphose
to the bluest of blues
when seen through the sphere
of a butterfly's eyes.

Jealous, he scours every tree
for the swallowtail-green,
spares the bright dust of her bloom
from the bruise
of the jar and the ether.
With index and thumb he fingers
her velvety thorax,
crushes her breath,
a slight nervy twitch
above his cheek.

He steadies the tip of a pin,
turning and turning her,
lifeless, suspended.

Chest-deep in swallowtail wings
he builds a great structure of gold
magnified one-thousand-fold.
In nano-spun platinum,
atom by atom,
he copies each cuticle-scale,
refracting the light on his wings
until her last trick is revealed –

and he sees with a butterfly's eyes.

Frigatebird

Floating, flesh going pink
in the warm
of the Gulf Stream,
arms and legs
spread out,
I saw the Magnificent Frigatebird,
red-throated in the sky,

his towering height,
his hungry beak
snatching and tearing:

a mighty albatross-man
to my seagull wingspan,
pinned out

for the man o' war bird
high above the water.

Roosevelt's Generals and the Long-Tailed Bats

Carlsbad Caverns, New Mexico, 1942

We watched you suckling your young:
holding your twins tight to your chest,
diving, wheeling, hunting –
strong as you were light –

we envied you your silent kill,
your mouth-suck chance to quietly cull,
select and take, and leave the husk.

Wings of leather in the night:
Oh my Reaper prototype.

And so we held you, thrumming, in our palms,
piled you in the planes in racks
of twenty-six on twenty-six

and with a little bulldog-clip
clicked a tiny bomb onto your chest
and set you loose.

The Witness

An Old Man's Voice

Geraniums

I remember the terracotta pots that held the geraniums,
and the smell of new paint on the windows and walls
when they cut off her hair that day.
The girls and the women smelled the paint smell
and it calmed them. Naked and quiet,
they laid clothes and shoes
by the pots that held the geraniums.

Testimony

When it was done the Ukrainians took long wooden poles,
each with a curved metal hook,
pulled each body in by piercing its mouth.
The dentists came then to tear out gold teeth.
I considered some time before watching at Belzec that day
to write up my hygiene report. I could not conclude,
on that day at least, that bodies
were disposed of in a sanitary way.

In the Museum

The voices run on a loop: an old woman
with numbers on her arm, talking of ripples and pools,
circles subsiding, memory a stone in its depth now.
I could not see clearly that day: steam misted the peephole.
I look through the glass now at the things we left behind:

broken glass from the cold beer we drank,
a pot for cooking, a bow for a dress,
grey buttons and spoons,
the red Bakelite thimble on the finger
of the fair-haired girl, broken now, cracked
by a stone or a foot; like the petals of geraniums.

Military Section,
Royal College of Surgeons

This is the skull with the soft fontanelles
that grew long ago in the womb of a woman
and pushed its way down and was blessed.

These are the sockets of eyes in the face
of a boy who tilled the green field.

Here are the splinters of bone in the hole
where his song spilled out onto grass.

Last Meeting

Harry Patch and Charles Kuentz, Ypres, 2004

In winter sunlight, here near France,
they wheel the last two out.

One by land, and one by sea,
so they may meet, these two,
and drink warm tea from cups half-full.
As if to spill a drop of tea
would make them weep.

And so they talk of this and that:
And you, he says,
and why did you?

And you, he says,
and why did you?

I had my orders too, he says.
You came at me with bayonet fixed.
In my dreams I see you still,
and hear the cracking of your bone.

There was a boy, he says,
whose name I never knew,
opened waist to shoulder by a shell.
He was beyond all human help.
And as he lay he begged us:
'shoot me', but was dead
before we could.

They drink their tea, eat biscuits from Alsace,
smiling now, together, here near France
they talk of how they each survived,
and ask each other's pardon
in winter sunlight in the garden.

The Floo'ers o the Forest

Jamie, Hawick, 2004

That's his kitbag lyin there.
I wonder if his shirt's folded square.

I ayeways hae tae turn his collar doun –
he's got that lang and lanky
cuttin gress an diggin gairdens.

The Airmy recruiters looked that smairt,
staunin bi the Horse an the Cross.

They let him feel the wecht o the gun,
telt him there wis mair
than cuttin gress an diggin gairdens,

offered him a trade,
said he'd see the world,
wear the Black Cock feather.

That's his kitbag.
The officer brocht it.

He said Jamie
fell wi honour.

He said I cuidna see him,
cuidna touch his hair
or turn his collar doun,

An I showed him the gairden
Jamie dug:

The grund, that broon and empty,
waitin for the floo'ers.

The Gamer

'Fire and Forget', Indian Springs, Nevada

She packs the Hershey's Kisses for the kids,
an apple and a plastic twist of raisins,
waves them off to school
beneath the green sequoia,

sips an ice-cold latte,
a moment to herself before the day,

picks up her watch and ID tag,
turns the blue Ford Taurus,
rolls the window down to breathe
the sagebrush on the way.

At the metal gate, she tilts her head
for the iris check,
the camera scans her eye,
and lets her in.

She sits down at her screen,
takes the joystick,
peers inside a land
of mirrored dust and shadows.

Two rooms precise,
exact across the planet,
her Reaper hovers,
soaring hawk-like from her wrist.

She follows one familiar silhouette,
spots the glowing cigarette,
she points and clicks,
drops 'Hellfire' where he stands:

a slick of blood and vapour
half a world away.

And when her shift is over
she takes them home
and holds them close
beneath the green sequoia,
and combs their hair,
and combs their hair,
and combs their hair.

At Sea

The signal on my phone is long gone,
the piano-man lulls me to sleep with a drink and a smile;
for a few dollars more he'll sing one for me
as I gaze at the black tugging sea.

The GI in dress uniform asks again for his song
as we sit side by side holding on,
remembering a roadside, and friends long ago,
between whisky sours and Long Island Iced Tea.

The girl with the willow-blonde hair
asks for only one song:
'Not tonight sweetheart,' the piano man smiles,
'it's way too sad for Christmas Eve,'
and follows her gaze as she leaves.

I slip into her seat, my long hair is curled,
my silk stockings seamed; a doodle-bug drones
and I'm down to my last cigarette;
the piano man lulls me to sleep
with Gershwin and Lerner and Loewe,
'It's Almost Like Being in Love,'

and I fold my dollars in the piano man's glass,
pretend he's smiling for me.

Entertaining the Emperor: Qin's Eternal Magician

Terracotta Army, Touring Collection

Other boys toyed with a ball and a cup,
a colt and a sword, a pup and a whip –
but Qin had the mould for my soul.

I was older than most –
no sure-footed warrior –
when Qin had me stand
in obsequious pose,
spinning my acrobat's plate
for the living and dead,

there with Qin's pot-bellied wrestlers,
the terracotta swans
and the worms
in his mercury garden.

Down on one leg,
I stood long and sore,
let Bi the potter steal my smile
and the style of my hair
to please Qin.

We spoke, as I posed,
Bi and I, of Gao Jianli,
of the lute player's tears of bright blood
running red from the place
where his eyes glistened once;

of the sound of the doors of a tomb,
the silence of shovels and picks
from workers sealed deep underground;

of Anqi Sheng's potion of youth,
of young men and girls
yet untouched,
lost to us now in their bloom,

and I look in your eyes
as you queue in long lines
just to watch me,

spinning the world on my finger,
watching you dying,
watching me living.

Killing America

I heard it, rising, chanting,
so close that I could touch it,

heard the raucous crying,
the raw-throated cawing:

I poked each flapping nest
until the red-winged blackbirds,
the scarlet tanagers,
the tree swallows
and the yellow warblers
were silenced.

Then I shot the New World quails,
the chuck-will's-widows,
the plovers and the egrets,
the bitterns and the purple martins,
until the woods lay quiet,
until the fear was gone
and the great lung
of the shining Okeechobee
breathed: breathed only for me.

Nansen's Ice Ghosts I & II

I

Ice (1888)

Fridtjof Nansen: Searching for the North Pole

For five months, alone together,
Nansen and Johansen
searched for the North Pole,
on through the ice.

Johansen cut the throats
of their sled-dogs one by one,
chose the weakest,
fed its body to the strongest.

Walrus fell to Nansen.
Their eyes haunted his sleep, bobbing,
wounded, from the ice, undead.

They pulled the bodies
from the water, cut through the skin.
The two men stank of blubber,
walrus grease and blood,
but they ate, thrived.

And all the while the *Fram*
drifted with the floe,
redrawing the map of our Earth.

II

Ghosts (2017)

She's left her land behind her, burning at her back,
hunger makes her desperate.
I am you, she mouths, *I am you*.
She freezes, fades, a sixty-second soundbite.
I watch her, warm in my living room.
She holds no piece of paper:
no pass, no refuge.

A hundred years ago, out of the ice floes,
the hand of a Nordic explorer took souls
from the water, half a million in his palm:

Stravinsky, Rachmaninov, Chagall, Pavlova,
refugees on Nansen passports.
They dance and they play for him still,
colour their fugues and concertos,
but not for us;
for us they die on the ice,
our ears deaf to their music.

Song for a Son

The leaves o yer tree are shinin reid,
green leaves tipped wi bluid in the sun.

They buried ye face doun in the nicht,
bade ye niver speak o the licht,

stapp't yer throat wi cley an wi glaur,
made yer grave a cowp fir their spoor

til naebody wuid hae kent ye wir ma son.
But they didnae see the seed in yer haun,

didnae see it root in the lime,
didnae see yer wurds rise an climb.

The leaves o yer tree ur shinin reid,
reid leaves singin oot tae the sun.

The Children's Tree

I

Punica granatum

In Isola San Giulio
at Elisa's palazzo,
if she lets you in,
you can climb the four steps
to the fleur-de-lys door,
lean into her garden for the *melograna*,
hold the tree's fruit in your hand,
all supple yellow leather,
fragrant-skinned:

those four ruby tears to tempt a daughter,
unformed still,

and October
just another word for summer.

II

Une grenade

In Rouen's ice-sheathed walls
the sun hides low in earth,
old men, women,
babies unbaptised –
les bouches inutiles –
pushed outside the gate.

Long enough to dream
in the siege of Rouen
of iron and blackpowder,
tight-packed in a bag:
twisted nails and thunder,
anything that cuts.

The supple leather
blazes red:
the first fruit of winter.

III

Throwing Overarm

The tendons of a boy's hand
poise then curl.

He bowls it
like he's been shown
with a straight overarm,

the shining cricket ball of childhood
turns and spins in Syrian light,

becomes *une grenade*
sweet-fleshed and ripe,

blazing red and russet,
the leather-skinned fruit
of the first frost
of winter

spins and turns,

the fuse burns,

explodes in a thousand seeds
and bitter flesh.

Winter

I want to be in part of the planet that's hot,
drinking frozen green lime margaritas
in Hemingway's house in Key West,
stroking the fur of a six-toed cat
that's called Frank or Errol or Marilyn
to the sound of a house-fan
that purrs with molecular heat.

I want to be cooling the sweat
of the sun on my legs
in the long crystal swathe of his pool,
breathing great gulps of moist air
as I rise and I fall in its pulse.

I want to walk out on Duval where the scent
of white jasmine still lingers,
watch Louisiana pelicans swoop
for silver-scaled fish
in the salt and the swell of the Gulf,

beat hard on the gong and the drum
at the going down of the sun,
celebrate each breath of red sunset
with bagpipes and brilliant bandanas.

Starlight from Saturn

I gathered up all of the waves,
the fountains of Ganymede's oceans,
flew through the ice rings to Saturn's lost Moon,
wet-faced and crying wind and rain.

I carved out a great crystal mirror: a prism
to shine back the past – a bright-flickered film
of poppies in iris-blue skies,
nectar-bees drowsed in the haze

of a day when mother wove coral
and seaweed and starfish and pearls,
and father found dolphins and sperm whales
and fish flying high on an indigo sea

in the blue luminescence of a planet
that breathed once, a moment ago.

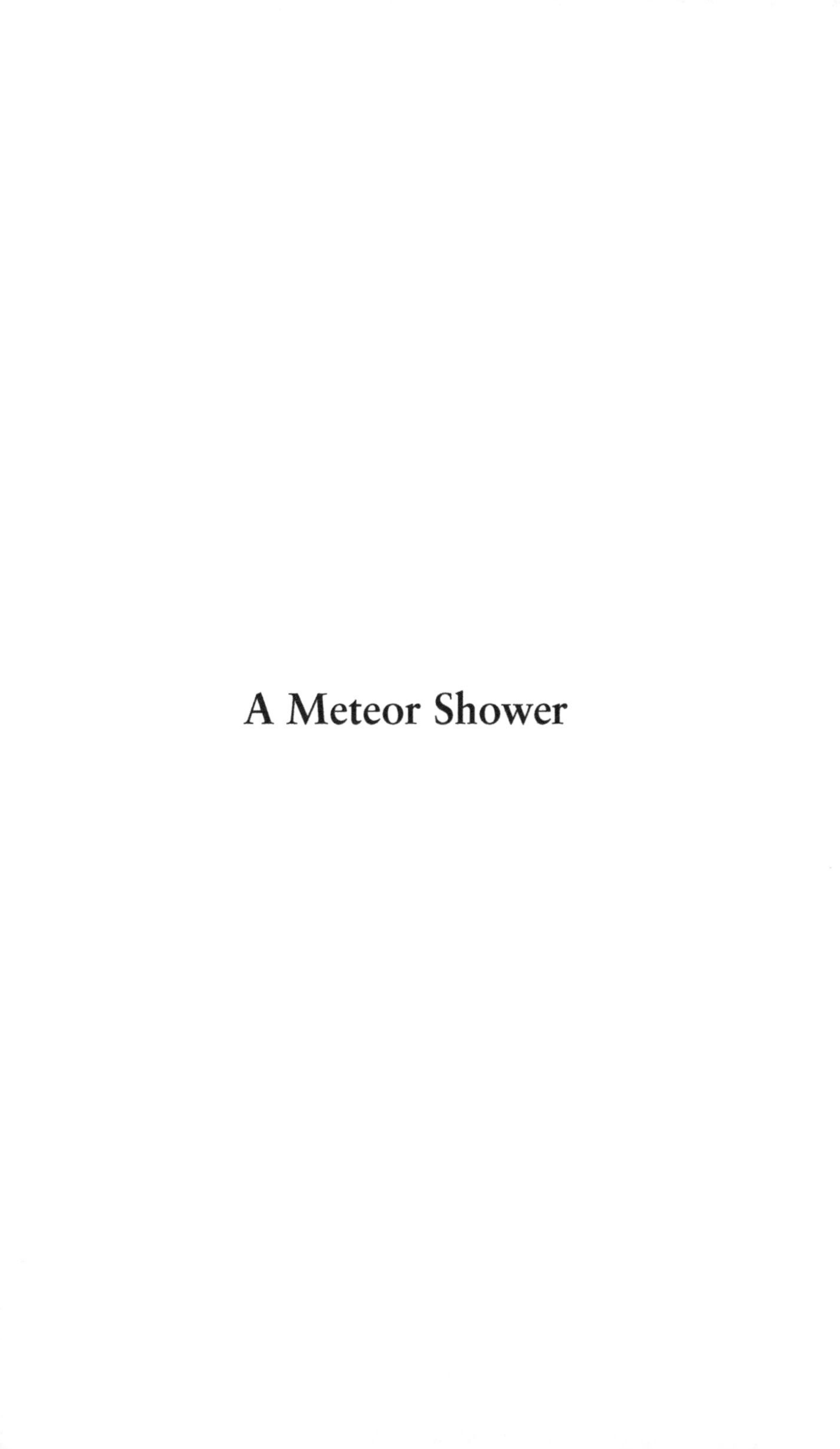

A Meteor Shower

Life Beyond?

For George Mackay Brown
(in response to 'Riddles of the Universe', from Under Brinkies' Brae)

Alone.
Sky scientist.
Human. Weaving his web.
Seeks significant other.
Soon please.

Apollo 1: Dress Rehearsal

Launch Complex, Cape Kennedy, Florida, 27 January 1967

History records them in training, praying at a table,
their heads bowed over a tiny white pyramid,

a mock-up of their module – a crew photo sent
to Apollo Spacecraft Program Office as a joke

by three who knew the price
of an electric spark, pure oxygen,

too much velcro and nylon,
and a door that opened in, not out.

Apollo 1: Guide Stars

Roger Chaffee, Virgil Ivan Grissom, Ed White II

They never tasted Moon dust,
never landed,

held their dreams of moonwalks
trapped in a burning module.

Their team-mates tell it slant,
remember them in NASA's guide stars.

Grissom snuck them through in '66:
Regor, Navi, Dnoces.

Angels' Landing

No wonder we dreamed there were angels,
flew to the sun on candlewax wings.

We risked all we had for this day,
a day when we soared and we spun,

far above Earth and its darkness,
touched every star never seen.

Voiceprints of an Astronaut: Last Men on the Moon I–V

For twelve who walked there 1969–72

I

Earthrise

That last night, when we slept on the Moon,
I woke to the sphere of the Earth, suspended,

a glassmaker's bauble blown
from the lips of a child: a light
in the dark of a dark with no end.

I want just to touch my own planet,
to hold each last mote of her dust,
safe-cupped and close in my palm.

If you could lie here with me
in the ash of the Moon's graphite-grey
you'd erase not one single Earth-line,
nor speck of coloured time,
nor bee's breath-weight of wind
with the hard edge of your hand.

II

Sleeping on the Moon

In the blackness of the blackness of the vacuum
I hear my spine unfurl,
singing in its lightness.

I try to sleep on the dark side of the Moon,
weightless in my hammock,
remembering
as we travelled through the black
I saw light

kindle

red

joining

      dot

to

dot

each flame a fire
each fire a man,
Nomad in Desert,
Aboriginal light,
holes of life on Earth.

I am thread
loosed from loom,
tug of chord
breath of womb

and I breathe my air,
sink my spine
in its lightness, singing
hammock-deep into dark,
and sleep now
with fire.

III

Amy

On the terrae of the Moon,
tired of coring rocks,
I slug Moon-stones into space,
do giant bunnyhops on film,
imagining her laughter
as my camera rolls.

And in the stillness of Moon-nights
I feel the tugging of the chord
to Amy's yellow nightlight
on the table in her room
and I trace out Amy's name
in grey-dead dust,

and I know when we come back,
to our footprints
and the stiffened flag,
Amy's name will still be there
in the sands without wind,
without tide.

IV

Earthbound

I stand here with the crowd
at Cape Canaveral now and then,
remembering that wet-ash taste of the Moon:
the silver lunar module
rises up on film,
legs asplay,
charcoal-grey

falling away

an image –
running backwards –
of a bug splatted at full throttle
on the windscreen of my car,
its spindle-legs askew.

Now and then, in winter sun,
I feel the thud of re-entry
boom and judder through my feet,
and I know they are back.

At home in my backyard
in the cold of winter
I look up:
hear my spine clicking,
remembering its lightness,

and on the silver disc above,
I know just where, in the windless stillness
I traced out Amy's name with my finger
in grey Moon-dust.

V

Lunar Sunrise: An Astronaut's Farewell (Cape Canaveral, Florida)

Had I known, I'd have held you
feather-slight in the crook of my arm,
flown with you from the place where *Apollo*
lights the night like the ascending sun,
where all the redfish of Banana River
leap and thrash in mid-air
and the core of Earth vibrates
at our leaving.

We would turn on the dark side of the Moon
to that single sphere of green and light
and watch our Earth rotate in cirrus clouds.

I would carry you to the Temple at Ephesus
and the Giant Buddha rock at Kiatang,
washed by foaming water at its feet.

I would hold your hand on Mount Omi
and the snows of Ruwenzori,
adorn your hair with shining tourmaline
and only then –

when we'd watched our Earth-sun rising
from the grey-dust of the Moon –

would I lay you down
by water's flow
where lilies grow

had I known it would end
with the plastic cup half-full
and the sheet
tucked too tight.

A Meteor Shower was Expected

Lines for Edwin Morgan
(27 April 1920 – 17 August 2010)

We weave him a sailboat of gorse and laurel,
daisies and rowan from the Kilpatrick hills,
carry him safe this late August night
in the storm of a planet that burned
for Bede and Columbus.

We peer through grey cloud
for the tail of the comet Swift-Tuttle,
through silver-spent rain from Perseus

to stars yet unborn in the blue
of the listening Pleiades,
where the plesiosaur swims, a jaguar weeps

and the meteor shower,
when it came,
was expected.

This is a photograph...

Family Album: at the Miners' Gala

Look how they laughed then,
the gang of them, before you and me,

lying on the grass,
their sandwiches and snowball cakes
held up for the camera,

my father at 20,
with his Fred Astaire hair,
stretched out his full length,
balanced like a Busby Berkeley chorus boy
on the shoulders of three girls.

His head is on Lillie
who will become famous
for her annual 'Jerusalem',
with her back to us all,
at Auntie Agg's New Year party.

His rib-cage is on Annie,
his cousin,
who will die of pneumonia
at her son's house in Bahrain,

and my father's bare feet
are on the shoulders of
Cathy,
who will be my mother,

who will throw back her head
in old age
to see the great lights
of the 10 o'clock Concorde
move across my London garden.

This is a Photograph of my Sister

The paint on the door
is peeling, bare wood shows through.
You're looking somewhere beyond me.
Your hair is jet-black, '50s-permed.
You wear a short cardigan, stretched
around a nurse's uniform.
Your hands brush my shoulders.
You're 20; I am six.

Two years from now, alone,
you'll climb down the steps
of the charter-flight from Prestwick,
an emigrant, old-style,
with what our mother
will always call
the nursing behind you.

You'll deliver a baby in a Toronto taxi –
but the taxi driver, not you,
will hit the headlines.
In 1963 you'll send home a picture
of someone who looks like Jackie Kennedy
in a nurse's white hat.
Only when we look more closely,
will we realise it's you: SRN, Toronto,
Western General Emergency Nurse.
My mother says she always knew
you'd go into *the nursing*
from the stitches you drew
on every doll you ever owned.

This is a Photograph of my Sister's House

In '81, your house has central vac.
You send us a picture;
the carpets are powder blue.
You've left *the nursing*.
Your husband dines on the tale
of the baby in the taxi,
you do admin in an office,
talk less and less.

You make your own vinaigrette
with oregano (stressed on the e),
coat chicken in Shake 'n Bake.
Maybe next year, he says,
he'll put in a pool.

Snow Angel: My Sister's Wings

2011

We found you in the garden
of the twenty-third house,
lying on your back,
legs and arms akimbo,

making snow-angels
like you did as a girl,
the white roots of your brown hair
startling now
in reflected snowlight.

Where's Hannah? you said.
I want to play with Hannah.

We brushed the ice off your blue nightdress,
warmed your freezing hands inside ours.
It's alright, we said, *we've come for you.*
We'll take you home.

But you knew, as you always did,
when we lied.

Motorhomes and Atriums

2019

Jet-lagged in the Marriott atrium,
long before their coffee's brewed,
I sit beside a crystal fire,
red-blue flames behind the glass,
clean fuel up an endless chimney.

The howl of the February wind skedaddles
between the downtown offices and banks:
Toronto, my sister's city.

The Toronto Blue Jays,
silent on the plasma screen,
Patsy Cline on the sound system.
A sleepless baby crawls
along the carpet near the fire,
her father humouring her.

You'd love this.
You'd know the baby's name by now
and where they were from,
have her quiet in your arms,
your nursing skills kicking in,
like always.

We drove from Toronto to Lake George once,
four of us in your oversized motor home,
the summer of '85.

The pair of us glued to *Live Aid*
and Bob Geldof,
picking up songs
from Wembley and Philadelphia
on the small TV all the way.
You slicing tomatoes and pickles,
conjuring sandwiches
between cupboard and counter,
perfectly balanced
on that long straight highway.

We'll laugh about it, I think,

then I remember
that you won't know
what I'm talking about.

I draw my coat around me,
catch the Go-train to the place
where they keep you safe and warm,
my hands deep in my pockets.

Out of her Depth

I float on my back,
holding her on my breast,

feel the small bones of her skull
cupped in my hand like a bird's,

her warm limbs relaxing,
yellow hair streaming,

a child swimming naked
on a turquoise-filled sea.

I move back from her,
my hands outstretched,

feeling the salt water tug
of the darkness beneath.

For Peggy

Peggy Ballantyne, Galashiels (1918–2011)

I want to remember
the five well-swept steps
to the glasshouse,

the lead crystal bowl
with the yellow tomatoes

and you on your knees
in the grass with my son

when the swords
were made out of paper

and the braw lads
came running home laughing
and sat at your table for tea.

Snow Apples

When the last leaf falls from my tree
three pock-marked yellow apples
cling to bare-bone branches,
fermenting from within.

At November's first hungry snowfall
a corbie dips its beak.
A magpie, upended,
lingers tipsy-tailed.

In the morning hard-frothed ice
seals the apple-husks
and the barn-owl wheels,
widdershins,
searching silent trees.

Walking with Death: a Pocketful of Posies

I will walk beside you,
insinuate, mutate:
staphylococcus aureus,
simian, *bovine*,
I can jump across,

BSE, SIV, HIV,
lavender's blue,
heliotrope cyanosis –
Spanish flu –
I was here before you,

I watch you as you love,
copulate, beget,
insinuate, mutate.

Watch you take your first breath,
watch you as they cleanse you,
a-tishoo, *a-tishoo*,
watch you as they bless you,

scrape off a cell from your cheek,
write out a blueprint that's *perfectly you*,
magnify me, amplify me,
sing a ring o' roses,
husha, *husha*,
watch the children play.

I was here before you.
You think that if you name me
I will go away?

Timeshifts: a Childhood

The ashes are bone-meal,
coarser than a human's.

They turn the leaves
of the corkscrew-tree mildew-white,

trickling down into calendula
and sticky willow weeds.

I hold the green cardboard box,
with a name, and an invoice with mine,

follow the instructions
to *peel and scatter*

then go inside
and watch the rain.

The shadow of a gold-haired spaniel
still appears now and then

in the rose and the bronze
and the green tones.

His long yellow ears gather
garlands of sticky-willow weeds

as he runs for red balls
in the buddleia bush,

and the laughter of a child in summer
echoes in cricket bats and swings.

I do not rush to clear them,
there will be time, enough.

Through a Lens in Winter

For Alastair

Before you were eight, my eye
was on the camcorder lens
at every school race that you ran.

I wanted to capture the green
of the green of the grass,
the light in your eyes
when you'd climbed to the top,
balancing high on the top of the hay,
the shape of the wispy-tailed cloud
you said was your lion,

that look on your face
when we first saw the world
from the cockpit with the pilot,

the sound of your laugh
when you rushed up the stairs
of each London bus
to bag the front seat and be driver.

But when I replayed
the camcorder film
in winter's first chill
all I could see was a smile in 2D,
and acres of empty blue sky

where I'd panned my lens far too wide,
chasing a hummingbird's wings
singing their song to the wind.

Asking

Great Torii, Miyajima

When the starlight's rising,
blooming on the red sakura,
I'll leave the crowds behind me,

hear the hushed wings of the Ho-oo,
land in silence on the Torii,

walk the tread of quiet deer,
swim the pathways of the seas.

There I'll wait, by Ama-no-Iwato,

with one dream only:
to ask you,
will you come with me?

Afterdeath

You sip the wine in that patch
at the end of our garden
where sun falls
till nearly November,

where you and I tilted
our faces to warm them
while he dreamed upstairs
of lightsaber battles
on far-distant moons.

The red plastic wagon you bought him –
the one that he filled to the brim once
with woodlice and leaves –
has bleached to pink,
covered over by ivy
in the buddleia roots
where he used to hide.

The stars are not stars here,
but flashes of light –
now and then I can see you –

the gooseberry wine on your lips
I can't taste,
the grey and black twist

of the curls on your brow,
I can't touch,

the leaves in our garden
the night we lay down there
after the rain.

I watch you asleep
in the bed where we loved,
watch till you waken,
and I leave you.

Fragments of Matter

We sailed out of Venice
when you were small,
past San Michele, the isle of the dead,
on to Murano where artisans fled
from Constantinople.

The glassmaker's furnace
was glowing white-hot
and he blew you an angel fish.

When I'm big I'll make you a flower, you said,
and you laughed as he turned a giraffe,
a tortoise, a cat and a porpoise,
held them aloft upon the *pontello*
to swirl and to colour them
cobalt and yellow,

then began once again,
breathing the world from his lips.

Second Creation

Roslin, Midlothian, June 1996

A scientist asleep on the floor,
waking each night on the hour,

keeping his distance,
letting the ewe have her space.

Twenty-nine dead or miscarried before:
the head much too big, the spark still too small,

blowing on a pinprick of blackened
red heat until it ignites into fire.

But the wonder, he says,
the wonder is that it succeeds at all.

The Loch

You will never hold me,
taste the things I touch,
blot me with the ocean,
seal my eyes from sight,
paint me grey-vermilion,
bruise my lips dark crimson,
for when the Earth was frozen,
bitter-hard,

I skimmed the loch
with a shaking hand,

split the membrane of the depth,
aureate in molten lead,
felt a tug of human kind,
a beating pulse inside.

Mary Queen of Scots: Beheaded

Maidservant to Mary Queen of Scots,
Fotheringhay Castle, February 1587:

They pulled ye doon tae yer knees, lady,
took aff yer kirtle tae shew that they cuid,
left yir white throat shilpit-bare.

In manus tuas, Domine, ma lady,
in manus tuas Domine, ma lady.

Ye kivered the white o yer hair,
yer hair that was yince rosey-licht –
white hair sae young in a lass.

In manus tuas, Domine, ma lady,
in manus tuas Domine, ma lady.

They spaittered the Skye terrier dug,
that hid in yer skirts, wi yer bluid.
An ah held the white lace in ma haun.

In manus tuas, Domine, ma lady,
in manus tuas Domine, ma lady.

Ah haud it, still warm, in ma palm,
bone-lace wreathed wi the scent o yer skin,
an ah'll say it for ye, ma lady:

In manus tuas Domine, ma lady,
in manus tuas Domine.

A Life

In all of our talks, when we spoke
of Iris Murdoch, and whether, at 30,
I'd ever considered the ticking of my clock,
I never once looked at your neck.

But your height and strong build,
and the taste of cigarettes,
and that smile,
came back yesterday

when I saw the notice of the auction
for Pierrepoint's tape measure
that counted the drop from the scaffold
in inches and feet, depending on height
and on weight

and on whether, as he noted in ink,
the neck was a *thick neck*, a *muscular neck*,
a *long* or a *feeble* or a *thin neck*;
or a neck that to him was just
an *ordinary* kind of a neck.

It was only years later,
as you cooked us dinner at your flat,
that I finally looked at your neck.
As we ate the strawberries you'd bought
you said, just this once,
I should break the habit of a lifetime.
'Try them with a little sugar', you said,
'to bring out their sweetness.
And listen to the ticking of the clock.'

In the Garden

For M

You saw it today: you gazed
at the apple tree's buds
like someone who never saw blossom
unfurl in the sunlight until now.

As light fades,
the blossom's a quiet silhouette.
I reach for your hand in the dark,

we lie on our backs
on the red tartan rug
we once used for picnics,
watching the holes
in the sky effervesce.
You tell me the night
has the chilled almond
taste of champagne

and you ask
if I'll help you to die.

We have no desire
for the cold prefab-blue
of Zurich, or Switzerland's snow.

I move the old stereo close to the window,
put *Fingal's Cave* on the turntable.
We can hear it quite loud
in the shade of the trees
at the foot of our garden.

I pour you the dose
in a clear crystal glass
well-laced with Bruichladdich,
sit down on the grass
and hum every note alongside you,
until only I
am singing.

Boy with Frog

Dorsoduro, Venice, 2013

Non toccare, says the guard
at Dorsoduro, *Non toccare.*

Each hand tries to touch
the beacon-whiteness of the child,
caress him like a diamond.

At the tip of the Canale Grande,
at Punta della Dogana,
his sparkle rises from the sift and silt
of palazzos' decay.

Look a little closer,
(hands behind your back
to keep the guard at bay),

no Michelangelo, no *David* this,
just a child
running naked from the water
to show you what he's found there,

his flesh silken milk,
his body white as the Moon.

At night they trap him in a net
of glass and steel and perspex
in case he flies away.

Room

I want to begin in a new-Moon room
with you
and the swing in the garden
waiting
for the girl with sweet limbs
to grow strong

and the walls, opalescent,
open to the wind.

Lockerbie, Pan Am flight 103

On 21 December 1988, the longest night of the year, Pan Am Flight 103 fell on the small town of Lockerbie in Scotland, killing all 259 passengers and crew and 11 Lockerbie residents. It remains the worst terrorist attack on UK *soil.*

The Wishin' Gate

Leuk beneath ma gravestane,
through the keekie-hole

when the rowan's laden,
when the summer's duin:

a skein o geese abuin me,
the green leaves muildert gold.

Divna come in warm July.
Come at winter's chill,

loose the boat aside the loch,
see the fire is set,

an touch the silvered lichen
by the wishin' gate.

Rescue Worker

21 December 1988

He can see them
where he found them,
lit by the beam
of the torch on his forehead,
untouched, it seemed,
by the fall.

He hoped
they had slept
but knew they had not:
those two young women
he found in the dark field
that December night

still strapped
to their plane-seats,
their arms
tight around each other,
their fingers crossed.

On a hillside

Human flesh hung on the trees at Tundergarth,
the day the sky rained limbs
and knives and forks
and tight-wrapped salt
and sugar-packs and hand-wipes.
And in the field, at Tundergarth,
the farmer heard the corbies caw.

Ruth saw a hand on her roof
and told the police.
Jessie made 200 scones
for the rescue workers.
Her dog fetched an arm
to the door
and she wrapped it in a cloth.

When the people came
from far away
about the t-shirts and the jerseys,
the notebooks and the backpacks
of the dead sons and daughters

that fell on Ella's house,
she gave them tea,
and helped them to find
their children's possessions.

And when the mother travelled,
with pieces of glass and sand
from the surfing beach
her son loved,

Ella helped her build a cairn
on the hill near Tundergarth
and sent her home,
different
from when she came.

Haud tae Me

Ella Ramsden's Poem

See the wey the sunlicht faas
abin the green floo'er oan the hill,
see the sun ye canna reach
oan that bit gorse aside the loch.

Haud ma haun an we will climb
up tae the licht there yonner.
See the wey, it's further yet,
further as we gan.

See the wey it lichts thon bit,
the bit ye think ye'll niver reach,

whaur iviry beuch o iviry tree's
in bloass'm fae the sun.
We will gan thigither there,
afore the summer's ower.

The boy who fell from the sky

Bunty Galloway's Poem

I was watching *This is Your Life* –
Harry Corbett. It had just started.

Then I heard it.
My whole house shook
like an earthquake,

I went out to the front
to get away from it.
He was just lying there
at the bottom of my steps:
a wee laddie in brown socks
and blue trousers.
At first I thought he was
just sleeping
so I put a lambswool blanket
around him.

He was there for day
after day. Nobody came
to take him away.
There were that many of them,
that many. A wee laddie
that fell from the sky.

The officers said they thought
they could maybe learn something
from the ways my boy landed.
It was that cold, that cold for the laddie.

I saw him every day.
In the end I said to them:
my boy's still there,
you've got to get my boy lifted.
And they came that night and they moved him.

And Christmas came and Christmas went,
but I never found out the name of *my* boy.

Toothpaste

It was the toothpaste that nearly defeated them.
It was there in each suitcase: each tube had exploded
over every shirt and blouse they tried to mend,

but one washed, one ironed and one folded,
until each trace of the blast,
of blood and of fuel was removed,
and at last, after seven years of waiting
the clothes of each son, of each daughter,
were returned to each mother, to each father,

and the unread pages of a journal
of a girl who lived to twenty
were unfolded, leaf by leaf,
ironed one by one,
her words returned
clean and washed in their pages.

Cameras

They laundered the t-shirts and jeans,
wrapped them in tissue,
sifted the scarves,
the London Bridge tea towels,
attached them to names,
wrapped them in paper
to send home.

They came to each small Instamatic,
its film tightly spooled.
They paused then,

fearful of light blanking faces,
of images blazed,

black turned to white,
left turned to right:

life's last celebration
wound in a coil in the dark.

Cakes and Scones

Emma, Josephine and Moira,
December 2018, Lockerbie

We knew it would be better if we did something.
We could go and help in the laundry,
but there were a lot of people – older people –
who couldn't come and do that. But they baked.

They would turn up at the kitchens with sponge cakes
and scones – just forever.

The school was inundated with everything.
I think the shops were emptied of vegetables.
But then the cakes and scones started,
and that was for the boys.

They needed something like that
to keep them going
because they were only boys,
because they were seeing terrible things.

Sometimes when they came in from searching,
they didn't want a meal,
just a few minutes to sit in the corner to think,
fifteen minutes and then get their heads around it.
Maybe a cup of tea and a wee something.

Rescuing the Rescuers

Angus's poem

How does the wind steal a man's belt?
How does the wind tear off a man's clothes
without leaving a mark?

All that death, all those bodies.
When I wake in the night,
wake in the night,

'How can the wind...

how does the wind

unthread a man's belt?'

The Town Hall: Colin's Poem, 2018

for PC Colin Dorrance MBE, aged 18, December 1988

She was the first one
we brought into the light.

The farmer drove up to the back door –
he had metal debris from the crash in his truck.

I saw a passenger on the front seat,
a young child, wrapped in a beige duffle-coat.

I thought at first she was a member of his family,
or a child he was babysitting.

He said he found her in his field,
that he couldn't leave her there.

He'd driven into town with her
She looked unharmed, light-coloured hair,

just a smudge of mud on her face,
but we knew that she was dead.

The telephone engineers, the electricians
were working upstairs

on high ladders talking, whistling
connecting phones, getting ready.

We carried her up the winding
stairs, two floors.

The men watched from the top
of their ladders.

They stopped whistling, stopped
hammering, stopped talking,

and one by one
all of them stood, silent.

Dark Elegy

Sculpture by Suse Lowenstein, Syracuse University, 2013

At Syracuse, the mothers
kneel in the snow,
their knees on the earth
where their young
walked once

remembering,
a young man's tread
on college steps, a young woman
unloading her books:
Philosophy, Theatre Studies, English.

Planted in each woman,
a piece of cloth, a shell,
a necklace, glass from a beach,
souvenirs fathomed in clay
deep in their wombs.

The Last Mother

2018

She wants to know about joy:
when he stayed up all night
in New York, in High School,
talking of God, or no God,
of jazz and Bruce Springsteen.

In London, outside his college classroom
she touches the iron railings, traces
their black fleur-de-lys shapes
with the palm of her hand.

In Edinburgh, at the castle, she lingers
under the archway – the one
in her son's picture by the soldier –

puts her fingers in her ears
for the One o'Clock Gun,
smiling, hearing what he heard,
she looks up, searching the blue
of the sky for her only child, trying
to imagine the sound of his voice.

747

As Strong as its Weakest Part

It was one small tear in the metal,
a pin prick in the skin of the Boeing.

The shock waves found the join,
the nose cone opened like a door,

tipping out its people
six miles high, free-falling.

Jigsaw

They are all waiting, remembering:

the fuselage, the cockpit,
the engines that spun
on the touch of a pin,
the portholes that showed us
the colours of Earth from the air.

The Gift

from Peter Geisecke, Park Place, Lockerbie
to Peggy Otenasek, Baltimore

The sky was too high,
too wide for her grief.

When Peter saw the American couple
at his garden gate in Lockerbie
he knew at once why they had come,
invited them in.

He gave Peggy the pebble
he'd used to mark the spot
on the hedge by his house
where her daughter fell.

Thirty years on, she waits by the roadside
for the rescuers cycling
to Syracuse from Arlington Cemetery.

She holds out her palm,
shows them the pebble.

It is what she has now:
a piece of the land
from the place
where her daughter fell,
where Peter found her.

A Card with Flowers

for the little girl in the red dress...
who lies here,
who made my flight from Frankfurt such fun
(Anonymous card on Lockerbie High Street)

When I fly now, I see you,
at airports, on plane-seats,
in line-ups and queues,
a child with skinny arms and red dress
drawing Mickey Mouse ears on the glass.

You open your book at the page
with coloured blocks that reach to the top,
and princes and kings in turret facades.

You examine each droplet of water
hugging your window's smooth edge
as wings lift you clear off the ground.

The droplets cling, run upwards,
your own private stream on the glass.
Ground disappears, and the clouds
are the colour of snow filled with light.

You unwrap your blanket around you;
your 5.00am start's catching up.
I reach for the pale plastic lip
of your blind, glad that it fits, exact:
a shield from the fire.

Teapots

The night before she fell,
Karen Hunt, 20, student,
packed her mother's gift:
an English teapot.

At Syracuse University,
the archives for the dead record it:
one gift of a teapot, bought
for her mother Peggy,
survived the crash.

Kim Cattrall, 32, actor,
running late, postponed,
took the next flight an hour later
to give herself time to buy a gift:
a Harrods teapot for her mother,
and lived.

How were they to know?
They flew for love,
flew for something that was new,
then flew again, to go home.

Beyond

Forward

Outside the town,
in Dryfesdale Cemetery,
Bryony's tree is right on the end.

My last name, a Borders name,
appears more than once here
in the local part of the cemetery.
I have lost no-one. Not here.
But Colin, out of long habit,
stands to one side, gives time to look, absorb.
He knows all there is to know
about needing a moment.

When he was on duty, at 18, beside the bodies,
he picked up a diary,
saw the last pages of December '88,
meetings penned in, plans
for New York, in Central Park, appointments
the dead woman beside him would never keep.
He stopped then, to protect himself, stopped
trying to join the dots of the story, until now.

We stop at Bryony's tree, bare of leaves in December,
bent to one side from the strong wind,
reaching towards the sky.

Tomorrow he will bring a young American woman
to this spot, and to the town's healed-over craters,
to see for the first time where her mother fell,
in her early thirties, a year older
than her daughter is tomorrow.

The Investigator

...But I have promises to keep,
And miles to go before I sleep...
(Robert Frost)

At Arlington Cemetery
on the longest day of darkness
the names of the dead
are intoned one by one;
an FBI man quotes Frost:
dark against light,
winter versus spring.

He lists the items he saw on the shelves
of a small wooden building in Lockerbie:
a teenager's single white sneaker,
a Syracuse college sweatshirt, never worn,
toys wrapped up for Christmas,
packed in the case of a father
who never came home.

Each charge is outlined with precision.
Robert Mueller has total recall
of all that was broken.
When the darkness falls again,
he will remember.

Terrorism: Changing the Playbook

FBI Victim Services Division, Washington DC

In Charleston, in 2015, the FBI found and returned
the clothes and the Bibles to the families,
to the loved ones, of nine black Americans
slaughtered as they prayed.

At 9/11, in New York, when the towers fell,
in Bali, in Paris, at the Boston Marathon,
at the Pulse nightclub shooting, Orlando,
the relatives and loved ones
were presented with their belongings,
washed clean of dirt and of blood by the FBI,

seventy-two of them, in a unit in Washington DC,
set up by Robert Mueller after seeing
the shredded clothes and possessions soaked
with blood, dirt and aviation fuel,
piled in a wooden shed in Lockerbie,

where he saw how the women of the town
cleaned them, folded them in tissue,
a new cloth wrapper,
paired them with handwritten names
and sent them home.

Notes on Poems

BIRD OF PARADISE

Tusitala: This poem won the National Portrait Galleries of Scotland Prize in 2011. The poem was inspired – in part – by the Count Nerli painting of RL Stevenson in Samoa held by the National Galleries of Scotland and also by The Writers' Museum section on Stevenson in the Lawnmarket, Edinburgh.

The Gamer: The AGM-114 Hellfire is an air-to-surface missile originally developed under the name 'Heliborne, Laser, Fire and Forget Missile'.

Nansen's Ice Ghosts: II, **Ghosts** (2017)**:** This was written as a commission for StAnza, Scotland's Poetry Festival, in 2017, in response to the Museum of the University of St Andrews' artefacts on the Norwegian polar explorer and diplomat, Fridtjof Nansen. Nansen was elected Rector of St Andrews by students there in 1925.

Nansen was the first to cross Greenland's inland ice – in 1888 – though he never reached the North Pole. In 1921, Nansen's humanitarian relief work on behalf of prisoners of war and starving people during the severe famine in the Soviet Union in 1921 earned him the Nobel Peace Prize. In 1922, Nansen became the world's first High Commissioner for Refugees appointed by the League of Nations – issuing 'Nansen passports' to stateless refugees to enable them to cross national borders.

Winter: Frank, Errol and Marilyn were among the many names of movie stars and performers Hemingway gave to the six-toed (polydactyl) cats living at his house in Key West.

Their six-toed descendants still live there today at the Ernest Hemingway Home and Museum.

VOICEPRINTS OF AN ASTRONAUT: LAST MEN ON THE MOON

Apollo 1: Guide Stars: During the Moon landing programme, 37 stars were chosen by NASA as guide stars, fixed reference points between the Earth and the Moon. As a practical joke, Grissom renamed Gamma Cassiopeiae, Gamma Velorum and Iota Ursae Majoris as Navi, Regor and Dnoces – Roger, Ivan and 'Second' spelled backwards. After the crew's death in a fire in their command capsule on the ground, these names were kept on the star charts.

Amy and Earthbound: Eugene Cernan, the last man on the Moon, traced out his the initials of his healthy daughter on the face of the Moon before he left.

An Astronaut's Farewell: *Did Neil take anything of Karen with him to the Moon?* Armstrong's biographer, James Hansen, asked Armstrong's sister, June. *I don't know*, she said. *I surely hope so.* (re. Neil Armstrong's daughter, Karen Armstrong, who died in 1962, at the age of two).

Asking: The mythical Ho-oo or hō-ō bird, the Japanese phoenix, is a messenger of goodwill and harmony that comes to earth and perches on top of the Torii, signifying new beginnings.

Ama-no-Iwato is the cave of the sun goddess, Ametarasu.

THIS IS A PHOTOGRAPH...

Mary Queen of Scots: Beheaded: *In manus tuas Domine* (*Into the Hands of the Lord*): Part of the prayer said by Mary Queen of Scots when she was executed. Her priest was at Fotheringhay Castle but was not permitted to see her. In her last letter, written at 2am, six hours before her execution Mary wrote to King Henry III of France, her former brother-in-law:

Tonight, after dinner, I have been advised of my sentence: I am to be executed like a criminal at eight in the morning. I have not had time to give you a full account of everything that has happened, but if you will listen to my doctor and my other unfortunate servants, you will learn the truth...
They have taken away my chaplain, and although he is in the building, I have not been able to get permission for him to come and hear my confession and give me the Last Sacrament. (Last Letter of Mary, Queen of Scots, held by the National Library of Scotland.)

LOCKERBIE, PAN AM FLIGHT 103

Cakes and Scones: Based on the words of Emma Pringle, Josephine Donaldson and Moira Shearer, the last three of the women in Lockerbie who carefully washed, pressed, folded and wrapped the clothes and effects of the victims so these could be returned to their loved ones. (Source: short film by the FBI, 2018.)

The Gift: In November 2018, 30 years on, Colin Dorrance MBE, together with other rescue workers and residents of Lockerbie, travelled to Syracuse University as part of the 'Cycle to Syracuse' event to raise money for a mental health charity for young people in Dumfries and Galloway. The lives of 35 Syracuse students lost on Pan Am Flight 103 are commemorated each year by the award of two Syracuse scholarships for Lockerbie students.

Forward: The word 'Forward' is the motto on the town crest of Lockerbie. The child handed over to Colin Dorrance MBE at Lockerbie Town Hall on 21 December 1988 was Bryony Owen, aged 20 months. Bryony and her mother, Yvonne, are buried in a single coffin in Pendine, Carmarthenshire, Wales.

The Investigator: Robert Mueller, now FBI Special Counsel, was director of the FBI from 2001–13. As acting US Deputy Attorney General, he was in charge of the Lockerbie investigation and indictment of Abdelbaset al-Megrahi, the Libyan charged with the Pan Am Flight 103 bombing.

The following poems in this collection have won first place in major poetry competitions:

Lockerbie, Pan Am Flight 103: 'Rescue Worker', 'On a Hillside', 'Toothpaste' – Mslexia, 2015.

'Military Section, Royal College of Surgeons' – the short poem category at Poetry on the Lake in Orta San Giulio, Italy, 2015.

'Tusitala' – National Galleries of Scotland Competition, 2011.

'Beheaded' – winner, Scots category, Wigtown Poetry Prize, 2012.

'The Floo'ers of the Forest (Jamie)' – Judges' and People's Prize, YES Arts Festival, 2013.

Luath Press Limited

committed to publishing well written books worth reading

LUATH PRESS takes its name from Robert Burns, whose little collie Luath (*Gael.*, swift or nimble) tripped up Jean Armour at a wedding and gave him the chance to speak to the woman who was to be his wife and the abiding love of his life. Burns called one of the 'Twa Dogs' Luath after Cuchullin's hunting dog in Ossian's *Fingal*.

Luath Press was established in 1981 in the heart of Burns country, and is now based a few steps up the road from Burns' first lodgings on Edinburgh's Royal Mile. Luath offers you distinctive writing with a hint of unexpected pleasures.

Most bookshops in the UK, the US, Canada, Australia, New Zealand and parts of Europe, either carry our books in stock or can order them for you. To order direct from us, please send a £sterling cheque, postal order, international money order or your credit card details (number, address of cardholder and expiry date) to us at the address below. Please add post and packing as follows: UK – £1.00 per delivery address; overseas surface mail – £2.50 per delivery address; overseas airmail – £3.50 for the first book to each delivery address, plus £1.00 for each additional book by airmail to the same address. If your order is a gift, we will happily enclose your card or message at no extra charge.

ILLUSTRATION: IAN KELLAS

Luath Press Limited
543/2 Castlehill
The Royal Mile
Edinburgh EH1 2ND
Scotland
Telephone: +44 (0)131 225 4326 (24 hours)
email: sales@luath. co.uk
Website: www. luath.co.uk